SHE'S THE ONE SHE NEED'S

STARLIGHT

Copyright © Starlight
All Rights Reserved.

ISBN 979-888530724-6

This book has been published with all efforts taken to make the material error-free after the consent of the author. However, the author and the publisher do not assume and hereby disclaim any liability to any party for any loss, damage, or disruption caused by errors or omissions, whether such errors or omissions result from negligence, accident, or any other cause.

While every effort has been made to avoid any mistake or omission, this publication is being sold on the condition and understanding that neither the author nor the publishers or printers would be liable in any manner to any person by reason of any mistake or omission in this publication or for any action taken or omitted to be taken or advice rendered or accepted on the basis of this work. For any defect in printing or binding the publishers will be liable only to replace the defective copy by another copy of this work then available.

I dedicate this poem to everyone who needs a gentle push towards breaking through the chains that trap them in their mind.

You all are equally wonderful, amazing and beautiful, don't forget that.

Don't let others define who you are and who you are meant to be, beacuse the only ones that can break these chains are you yourselves.

Keep fighting for what you want and for what you believe is right, and all your dreams will come true.

Contents

Preface

This poem is about a girl who is trapped in her own mind, who wants to break free of the chains that bind her. But the only one who can do that is the girl herself.

It is also about her feeling and her thoughts.

1. She's The One She Needs

There are times that she wonders
Is she deserving,
of the life she lives.
She wonders
If she must confine herself,
To rid them all
From the burden
That she causes
With her existence.
Sometimes she wonders,
If anyone will be able
To see past the mask
That she puts on to make them smile,
To make them believe,
That she is happy.
She tries to break through
The chains of her sadness
And let go.
But is afraid of the disappointment
Of the people she loves,
That she is not what they want.
She feels burdened

By the guilt she harbors,
For the anger she shows to her family,
Because she doesn't know
Why they even want her.
She knows that she is undeserving
Of the love that she receives.
She tries to shun her thoughts
Of not being good enough,
For being a waste of space.
She tries to give and give to everyone,
Scared that they will let go
If she stops to ask for herself.
She feels trapped
In the confines of her own heart.
Wanting to shout
That she too wants
What they all seem to have.
To have a pinch of the kindness
That she spreads,
To have a piece of the cake
That everyone but her seems to tasted,
To have that shoulder to cry on,
To have someone who will listen
To her woes,
To have a that lighthouse
That will guide her,
To have one who will aid her

In calming the storm of emotions
That she bears deep within her soul,
To have someone
Who will help her mend
The cracks that she has on her spirit,
To break herself free,
But she can rely on
Only one such individual,
For the only one
Who can breaks these chains
Is she herself.

2. She's The One She Needs To Believe

She is a humble soul
Who gave her all
To everyone and everything that she did
She is a mixture of all that is good
And yet why must she get hurt
For the sins she has not committed
For every accusing finger
That rises against her
She must stand tall
And she must stand proud
For she is the one she needs to believe
Not the liars who always flee
She can break through these chains that bind her
For she knows that it is not she who has sinned
She doesn't need anyone else
To believe her
To help her rise
For she is the only one she needs
And she is the only one she needs to believe

3. She's The One She Needs To Be

She wonders why she must change
To please those around her
She wonders what her weight has to do
With what she wishes to accomplish
She wonders why she has to change
Her opinion
Just because no one accepts it
Why must she bend over backwards
Just to fit in with the crowd
Why can't she stand out
And be who she wants to be
Why must she change her style to fit in
Why must she change her body to be loved
Why must the world change her spirit
She is most beautiful
When she is herself
For she is the one she needs to be
She need not be an artificial porcelain doll
To shine her bright light
All she must do, is be true
Her light shines brighter when she smiles
From ear to ear

She needs to love who she is
For only she herself
Can put a smile on her face.
For being true to who she is
Is all she needs to do
For she is the one she needs to be
To always shine soo brightly

www.ingramcontent.com/pod-product-compliance
Lightning Source LLC
Chambersburg PA
CBHW072155150726
48002CB00004B/1678